Journey to
Pennsylvania

Written & Illustrated by

Josh VanBrakle

Arboreal Press

Arboreal Press
Hummelstown, PA 17036

ISBN-13: 979-8-9991586-0-4

First Edition: 2025
10 9 8 7 6 5 4 3 2 1

Have many adventures.

The Mystic Land of Pennsylvania

Welcome, traveler, to Pennsylvania! This land abounds in history, nature, people, and more. Let us explore this wondrous state in a journey—a journey to Pennsylvania.

Pennsylvania Fast Facts

Abbreviation: PA
Nickname: Keystone State
Joined US: 12/12/1787 (2nd)
Capital: Harrisburg
Size: 46,058 square miles (33rd)
Population: 13 million (5th)
Flag:

Did You Know?

Pennsylvania's nickname refers to the central stone in an arch, which holds all the other stones in place. Pennsylvania is the "Keystone State" because it played a central role in founding the United States.

Pennsylvania County Map

NEW YORK

MARYLAND

WEST VIRGINIA

VIRGINIA

NEW JERSEY

DELAWARE

Lake Erie

Erie

ERIE

CRAWFORD

WARREN

MCKEAN

POTTER

TIOGA

BRADFORD

SUSQUEHANNA

WAYNE

VENANGO

FOREST

ELK

CAMERON

MERCER

LACKAWANNA

Scranton

PIKE

CLARION

JEFFERSON

CLEARFIELD

CLINTON

LYCOMING

Williamsport

SULLIVAN

WYOMING

Wilkes Barre

Punxsutawney

CENTRE

UNION

MONTOUR

COLUMBIA

LUZERNE

Hazleton

CARBON

MONROE

BUTLER

ARMSTRONG

INDIANA

State College

SNYDER

NORTHUMBERLAND

SCHUYLKILL

NORTHAMPTON

Bethlehem

Easton

BEAVER

ALLEGHENY

MIFFLIN

JUNIATA

Altoona

BLAIR

CAMBRIA

Allentown

LEHIGH

Pittsburgh

WASHINGTON

Johnstown

WESTMORELAND

HUNTINGDON

PERRY

DAUPHIN

LEBANON

Hershey

BERKS

Reading

BUCKS

GREENE

FAYETTE

SOMERSET

BEDFORD

FULTON

Harrisburg

CUMBERLAND

MONTGOMERY

FRANKLIN

York

Lancaster

LANCASTER

CHESTER

Philadelphia

DELAWARE

ADAMS

Gettysburg

YORK

LAWRENCE

Allegheny River

West Branch Susquehanna River

Susquehanna River

Juniata River

Beaver River

Ohio River

Monongahela River

Chesapeake Bay

Delaware Bay

79

80

376

76

78

81

83

70

84

380

476

276

Four Regions of Pennsylvania

Pennsylvania has a diverse landscape. It has four regions, each with its own terrain. Using the map on the right, can you spot what makes each region different?

Did You Know?

The Erie Drift Plain has gentle hills and farms along Lake Erie, one of the Great Lakes.

A "plateau" is an area of high, flat ground. The Allegheny Plateau used to be that way, but it's so old that water has worn it away.

The Pennsylvania Appalachians are also called the "Ridge and Valley" region. You can see on the map how all the hills fold on top of each other.

A "piedmont" is a flat area at the base of mountains. Pennsylvania's Piedmont has some of the best farmland in the U.S.

LAKE ERIE

Erie ▲

ERIE
DRIFT PLAIN

ALLEGHENY PLATEAU

Scranton ▲
Wilkes Barre ▲

Williamsport ▲

State College ▲

Pittsburgh ▲

Altoona ▲

Johnstown ▲

APPALACHIAN MOUNTAINS

Allentown ▲

Harrisburg ★

York ▲

Lancaster ▲

Philadelphia ▲

PIEDMONT

The First Pennsylvanians

People have lived in Pennsylvania for at least 12,000 years. Most of that time, Native Americans controlled the state.

Many tribes lived in Pennsylvania. Who lived where changed over time, and territories often overlapped. This map shows simplified tribal ranges prior to European arrival.

More than 50,000 Native Americans live in Pennsylvania today, according to the U.S. Census. Native American language endures in many Pennsylvania place names, especially rivers. You can see some of these places on the map.

Did You Know?

Lenni-Lenape Chief Lappawinsoe was the first Native American portrayed in an oil painting. He had his picture painted in 1735.

LAKE ERIE

Erie

Allegheny R.

Susquehanock

Lycoming Cr.

Tunkhanock

Lackawaxen R.

Lackawaxen R.

Munsee Lenape

Sinnemahoning Cr.

Punxsutawney

ALLEGHENY MTNS

Mount Nittany

Susquehanna R.

Nescopeck

Wapwallopen

Conoquenessing Cr.

Aliquippa

Kittaning

Monongahela

Conemaugh R.

Shamokin

Shenandoah

Catasauqua

Lehni-Lenape

Ohio R.

Loyalhanna Cr.

Juniata R.

Wiconisco Cr.

Tulpehocken Cr.

Tinicum Cr.

Perkiomen Cr.

Youghiogheny R.

Swatara Cr.

Monongahela R.

Ohiopyle

Conewago Cr.

Conestoga R.

Conshohocken

Wissahickon

Conodogwinit Cr.

Mackinipattis Cr.

Ye Olde Pennsylvania

In 1681, King Charles II of England granted William Penn a colony to pay a debt. The king named the colony "Pennsylvania" or "Penn's Woods" in honor of Penn's father.

Unfortunately, Penn's grant overlapped other colonies. Connecticut, Maryland, New York, and Virginia all had claims to parts of Pennsylvania.

The differences led to violence. In the 1730s, Maryland and Pennsylvania battled in Cresap's War. Two surveyors, Charles Mason and Jeremiah Dixon, brought peace in 1767 by marking a compromise border. That border, the Mason-Dixon Line, later became famous as the divide between North and South in the U.S. Civil War.

Did You Know?

William Penn (left) wanted Pennsylvania to have ocean access, so in 1682 he leased Delaware from the Duke of York. Delaware was part of Pennsylvania until 1776, when Delaware formed its own state.

The darker color on this map shows Pennsylvania's original land. Today's state lines are also shown to reveal how the borders changed.

Lake Erie

New York

Ohio

New Jersey

Mason-Dixon Line

Maryland

New Jersey

West Virginia

Virginia

Delaware

Pennsylvania...Deutch?

Some of William Penn's first colonists were refugees. Germans fled to Pennsylvania to escape wars in Europe. These "Deutch" became known as Pennsylvania Dutch, even though they weren't Dutch at all.

At one time, Pennsylvania Dutch made up half of Pennsylvanians. Many still live in the state's southeastern counties.

The Pennsylvania Dutch have some unique customs. One is painting barns with round signs, called hex signs, to ward off evil. This page's map of Pennsylvania Dutch Country is modeled on real hex sign colors.

Did You Know?

The best-known Pennsylvania Dutch are the Amish. Amish religion promotes a simple life. They wear basic clothes, farm the land, and avoid technology, including cars.

*Bless*this*map*

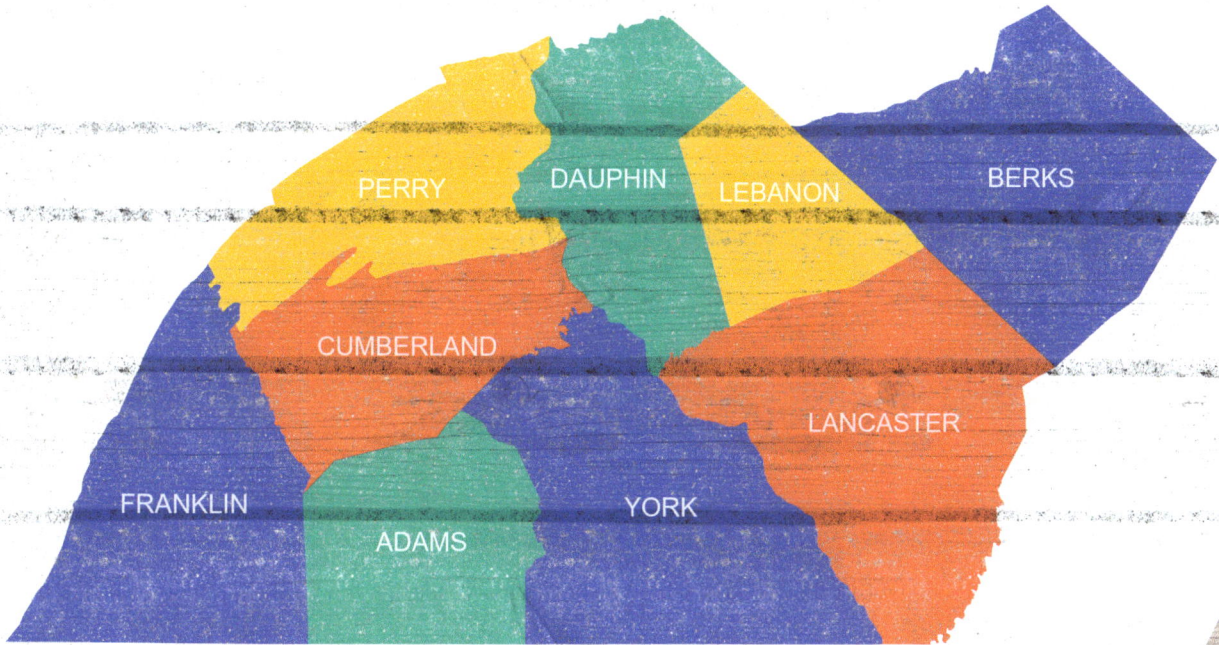

PERRY

DAUPHIN

LEBANON

BERKS

CUMBERLAND

LANCASTER

FRANKLIN

ADAMS

YORK

Sites in Pennsylvania History

Pennsylvania has played a central role in U.S. history. Both the Declaration of Independence and U.S. Constitution were written here. Pennsylvania was also the turning point of the U.S. Civil War. Without the Union victory at the Battle of Gettysburg, the U.S. might not exist today.

Pennsylvania has plenty of fun history too. It's the state with the first U.S. zoo, roller coaster, and Little League baseball game. It's even the birthplace of the banana split!

Did You Know?

On September 11, 2001, passengers on United Airlines Flight 93 prevented a terrorist attack on the U.S. Capitol. The plane crashed in a Pennsylvania field instead. The Tower of Voices in Stoystown honors these heroes. The 93-foot sculpture has 40 wind chimes, one for each passenger and crew member killed.

Erie
Flagship USS Niagara built (1812)

Titusville
First oil well drilled (1859)

Williamsport
First Little League baseball game played (1939)

Jim Thorpe
First US roller coaster (1850s)

Pittsburgh
Polio vaccine developed (1953)
Can pull-tab invented (1962)

Latrobe
Banana split invented (1904)

Harrisburg
Becomes PA's state capital (1812)

Middletown
Three Mile Island nuclear accident (1979)

Philadelphia
First US hospital (1751)
capital (1774)
zoo (1874)

Stoystown
Flight 93 crashes (2001)

Gettysburg
Battle of Gettysburg (1863)

Hanover
First US Civil War battle north of Mason-Dixon Line (1863)

Chadds Ford
Battle of Brandywine (1777)

Made in Pennsylvania

Look at the "heads" side of a U.S. coin. See that letter in the lower right? It tells you where the coin was made. A "P" means the coin came from Philadelphia.

Coins are just one of many things that come from Pennsylvania. The state has North America's largest chocolate maker, Hershey. It grows 70% of all U.S. mushrooms and bakes 80% of all U.S. pretzels. From Slinkies to snowboards, crayons to candies, it's made in PA.

Did You Know?

Pennsylvania is a big farming state. Besides mushrooms, it also ranks in the top ten U.S. states for apples, milk, grapes, and Christmas trees.

Get OUT(side) in Pennsylvania

Pennsylvania's diverse terrain makes it a popular place to enjoy nature. The state has more than 14,000 miles of trails, including part of the famous Appalachian Trail. Add in over 2,000 miles of state water trails, and you'll never run out of routes to explore.

Did You Know?

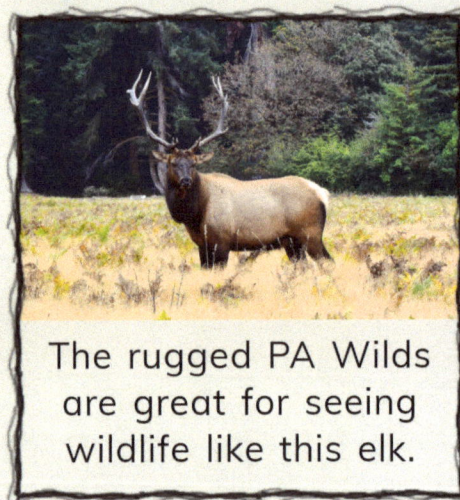

The rugged PA Wilds are great for seeing wildlife like this elk.

The Allegheny, Ohio, and Monongahela Rivers meet in Pittsburgh—perfect paddling.

Pennsylvania's many caverns let you explore nature underground.

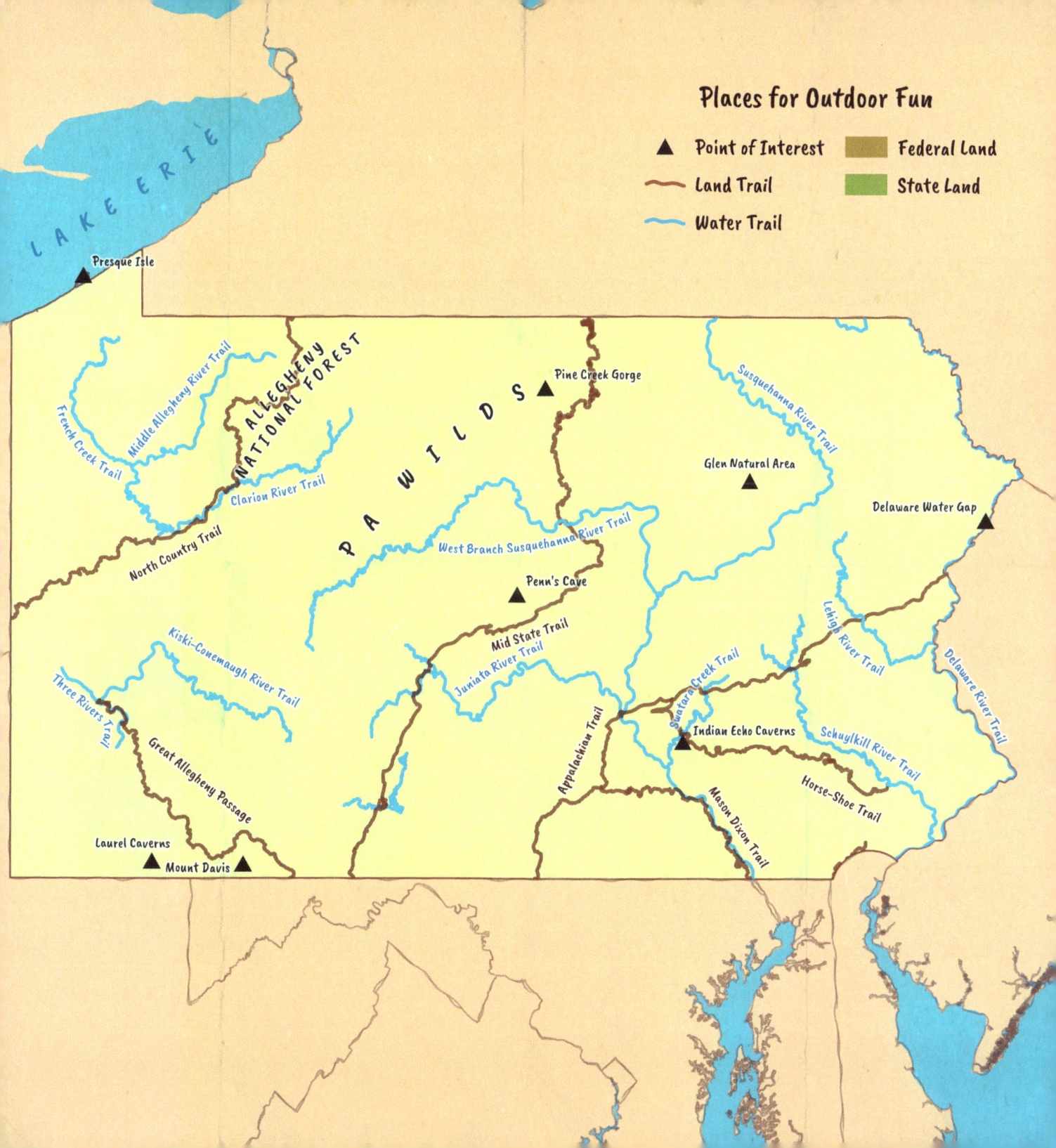

Places for Outdoor Fun

▲ Point of Interest

— Land Trail

— Water Trail

Federal Land

State Land

LAKE ERIE

▲ Presque Isle

ALLEGHENY NATIONAL FOREST

PA WILDS

French Creek Trail

Middle Allegheny River Trail

Clarion River Trail

North Country Trail

▲ Pine Creek Gorge

Susquehanna River Trail

▲ Glen Natural Area

▲ Delaware Water Gap

West Branch Susquehanna River Trail

▲ Penn's Cave

Mid State Trail

Juniata River Trail

Lehigh River Trail

Delaware River Trail

Kiski-Conemaugh River Trail

Three Rivers Trail

Great Allegheny Passage

Appalachian Trail

Swatara Creek Trail

▲ Indian Echo Caverns

Schuylkill River Trail

Horse-Shoe Trail

Mason Dixon Trail

Laurel Caverns ▲   ▲ Mount Davis

😆 Weird & Wacky Towns 😆

Pennsylvania has more than its share of bizarre town names. From Big Beaver to Bath Addition, check out these strange places.

Did You Know?

Chinchilla really is named after the adorable rodent.

Business District, Wyoming Avenue, Forty Fort, Pa. K-10

Forty Fort in 1940 (of course!). It got its name because forty people built a fort there in 1770.

No, I don't know how Elk Lick got its name. And no, I do not <u>want</u> to know how Elk Lick got its name.

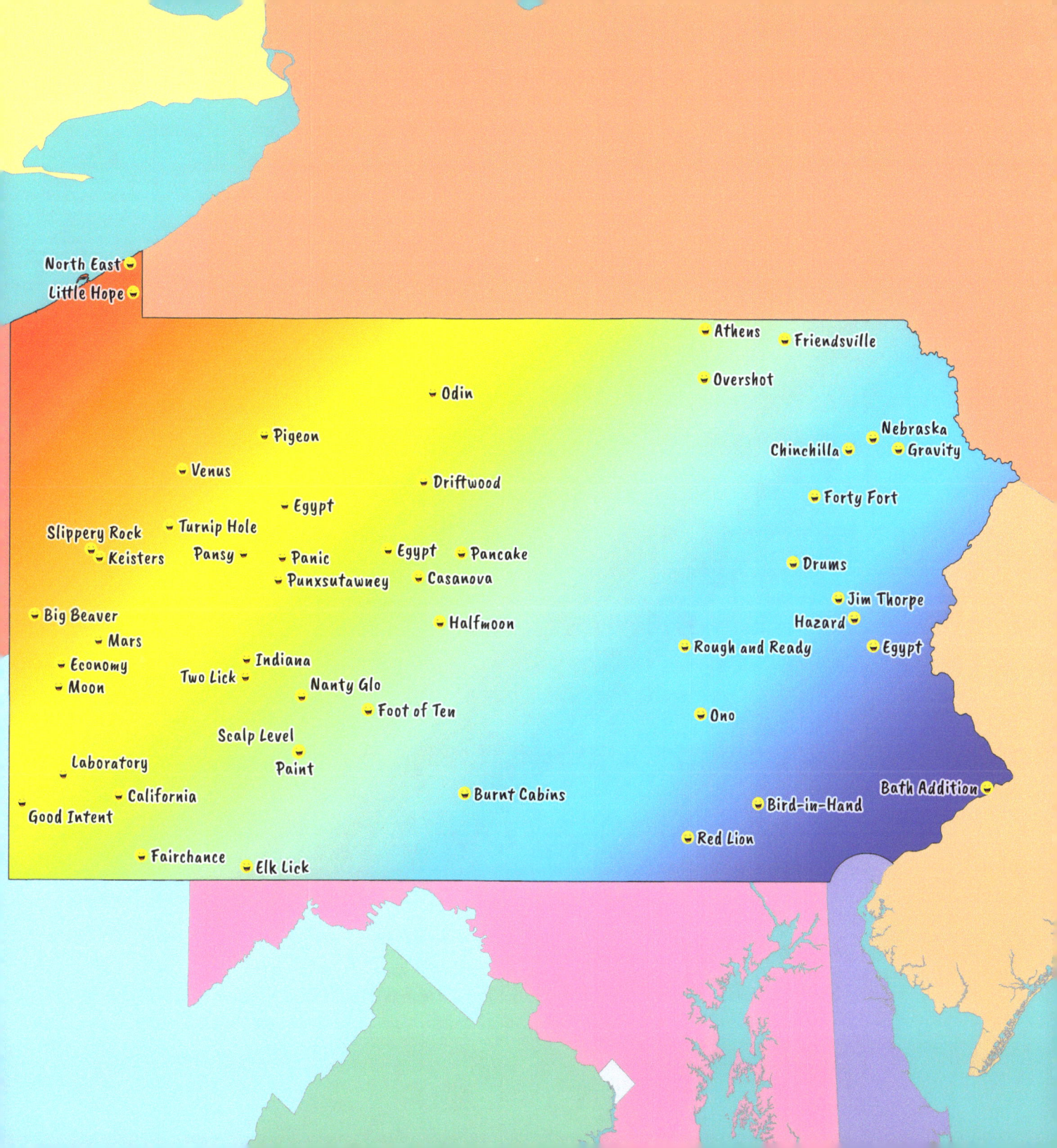

North East

Little Hope

Athens

Friendsville

Overshot

Odin

Nebraska

Pigeon

Chinchilla

Gravity

Venus

Driftwood

Forty Fort

Egypt

Slippery Rock

Turnip Hole

Keisters

Pansy

Panic

Egypt

Pancake

Drums

Punxsutawney

Casanova

Jim Thorpe

Big Beaver

Halfmoon

Hazard

Mars

Indiana

Rough and Ready

Egypt

Economy

Two Lick

Moon

Nanty Glo

Foot of Ten

Ono

Scalp Level

Laboratory

Paint

California

Burnt Cabins

Bath Addition

Good Intent

Bird-in-Hand

Fairchance

Elk Lick

Red Lion

PHILADELPHIA
City of Brotherly Love

Philadelphia is Pennsylvania's largest city. More than 1.5 million people live here! That makes Philadelphia the fifth largest city in the U.S.

When it comes to U.S. history, there are few better places to visit than Philly. It was the first U.S. capital. It's where the Declaration of Independence was signed and the U.S. Constitution was written. No wonder another nickname for Philadelphia is "America's Birthplace." Grab a cheesesteak and stroll through the past.

Did you know?

Independence National Historical Park is the spot to go for history in Philadelphia. In a few blocks you'll see Independence Hall (left), the Liberty Bell (middle), Congress Hall (right), and more.

Miles

0 ½ 1   2   3   4

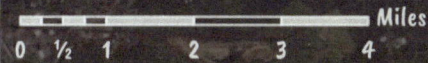

Morris Arboretum

Benjamin Rush
State Park

532

63

Pennypack
Park

Wissahickon
Valley Park

309

73

Tacony
Creek Park

1

13

95

1

76

Fairmount
Park

Philadelphia Zoo

30

Eastern State Penitentiary

95

Cobbs
Creek Park

Philadelphia Museum of Art

3

Franklin Institute

13

676

Reading Terminal Market

Independence
National
Historical Park

John Heinz
National Wildlife
Refuge At Tinicum

Schuylkill River

Citizens Bank Park

76

Wells Fargo Center

291

F.D.
Roosevelt
Park

Lincoln Financial Field

95

Philadelphia International Airport

Delaware River

PITTSBURGH
Steel City

Pittsburgh started as a military fort. It guarded a vital spot in western Pennsylvania where three rivers meet. Later it became the center of U.S. steel making. In the early 1900s, half of U.S. steel came from Pittsburgh.

Modern Pittsburgh has lost much of its steel making, but the city is having a rebirth. It has become a technology hub. Leaders in artificial intelligence, robotics, and self-driving cars are among the 1,800 tech companies operating in the city.

Did You Know?

The hills south of the Monongahela River offer great downtown views. Climb aboard the Duquesne Incline and get your camera ready.

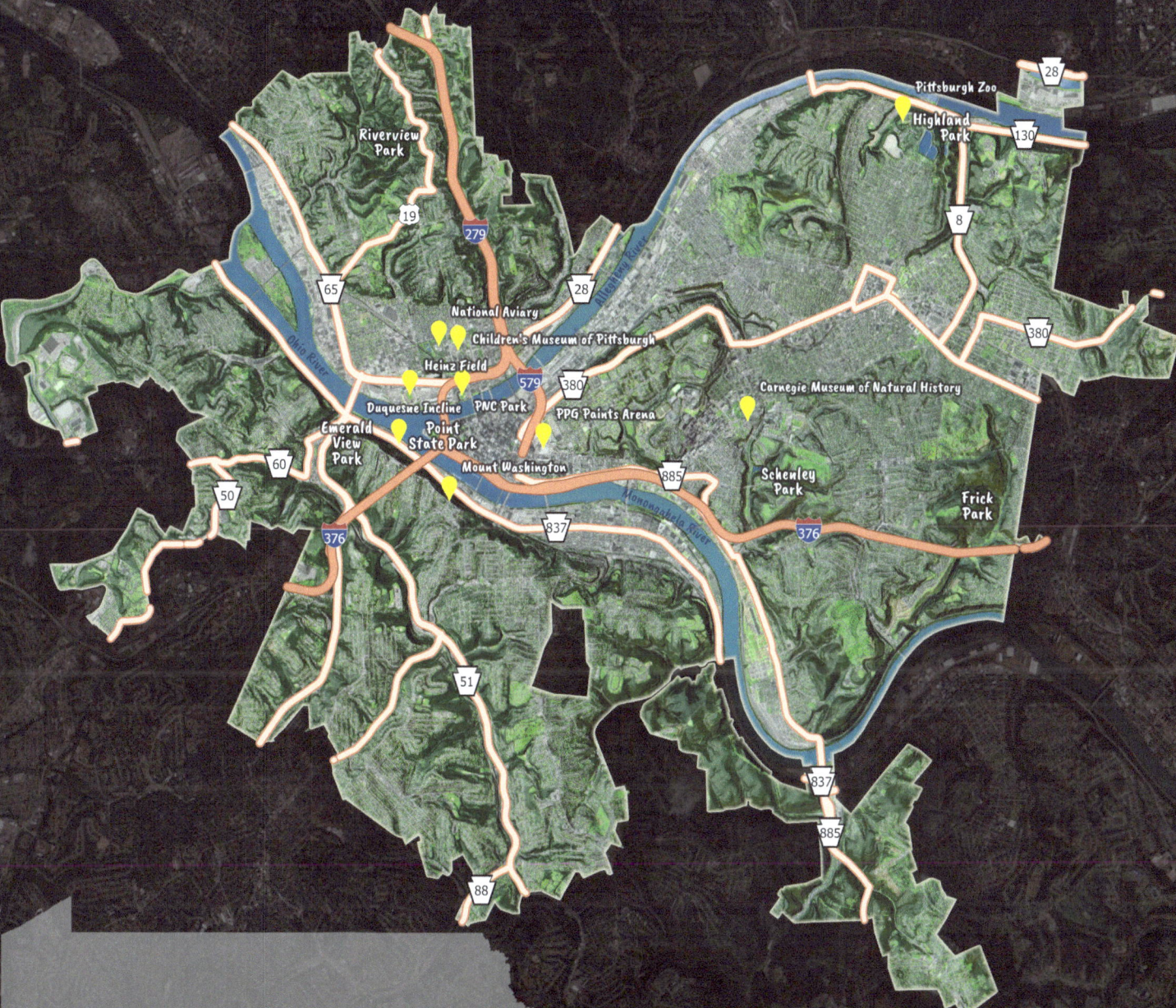

Riverview Park

Pittsburgh Zoo

Highland Park

National Aviary

Children's Museum of Pittsburgh

Heinz Field

Carnegie Museum of Natural History

Duquesne Incline

PNC Park

PPG Paints Arena

Emerald View Park

Point State Park

Schenley Park

Mount Washington

Frick Park

Ohio River

Allegheny River

Monongahela River

0   ½   1   2   3

Miles

HARRISBURG
State Capital

Philadelphia and Pittsburgh may be larger, but Harrisburg is Pennsylvania's capital. The city is located in the middle of the state along the Susquehanna River. This central location was the reason Harrisburg became the state's capital in 1812.

Despite its small size, Harrisburg packs a lot in. Museums, historic sites, and the state capitol make the city worth a visit. Walking paths along the Susquehanna provide a break from downtown crowds. For the adventurous, many of the wooded river islands are open for camping.

Did You Know?

The state capitol building in Harrisburg hosts free guided tours seven days a week.

Goodnight, Pennsylvania

Our Pennsylvania journey has reached its end, but <u>your</u> journey can continue. Never stop exploring. Have many adventures.

WANT TO KEEP EXPLORING PENNSYLVANIA? TRY THESE WEBSITES:

Pennsylvania State Museum - statemuseumpa.org

Pennsylvania Capitol - pacapitol.com

Independence National Historical Park - nps.gov/inde

Visit PA - visitpa.com

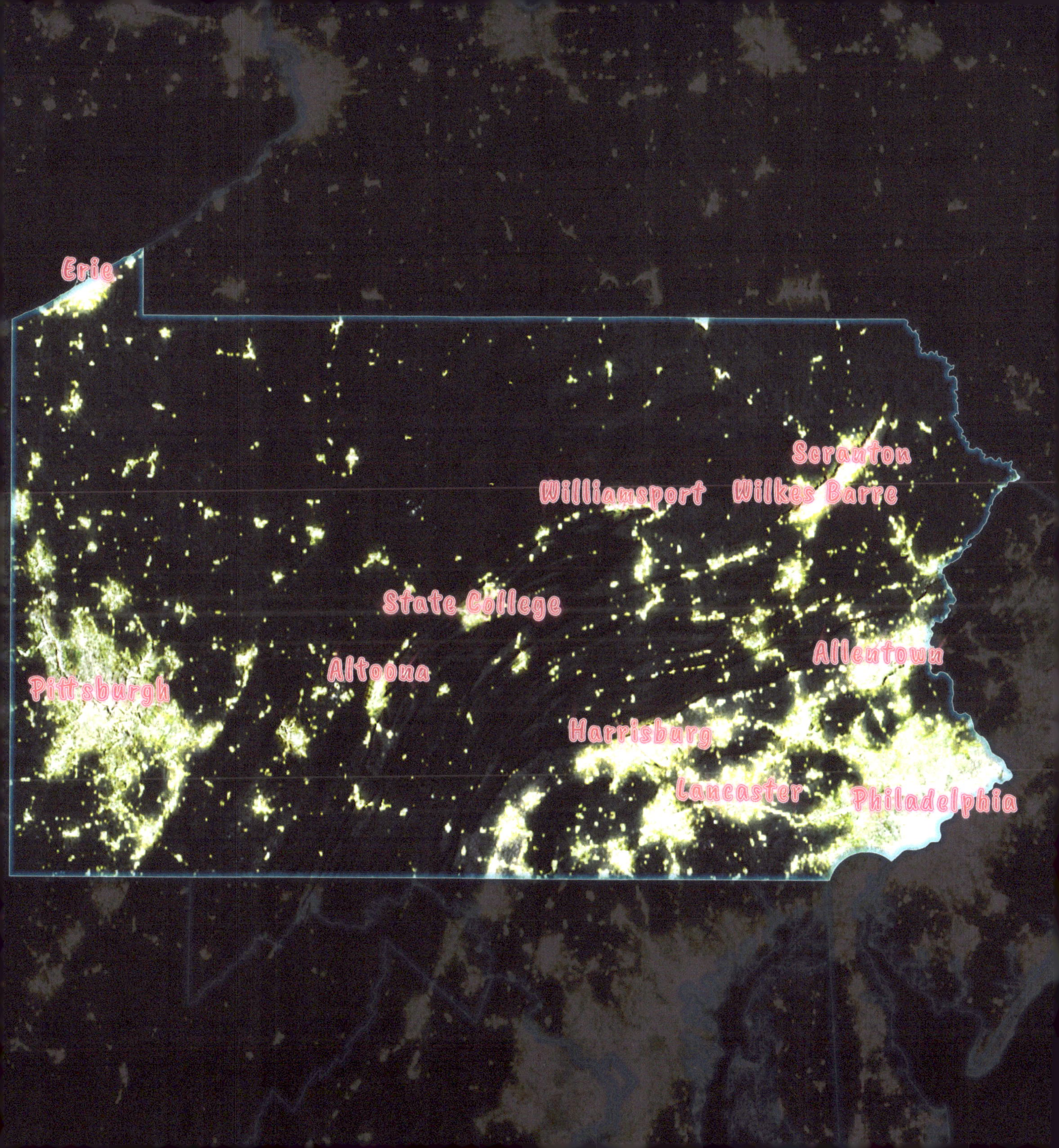

Erie
Scranton
Williamsport
Wilkes Barre
State College
Allentown
Altoona
Pittsburgh
Harrisburg
Lancaster
Philadelphia

www.ingramcontent.com/pod-product-compliance
Lightning Source LLC
Chambersburg PA
CBHW042106040426

42448CB00002B/168